AF571885

ALLUVIAL

The Bucknell Series in Contemporary Poetry

This is one of a limited number of books of poetry of the highest quality published annually by the Bucknell University Press, in conjunction with *West Branch Literary Journal* and the Stadler Center for Poetry.

Titles in This Series

Karl Patten, *Touch*
Afaa Weaver, *The Ten Lights of God*
Charles Borkhuis, *Alpha Ruins*
Harryette Mullen, *Tree Tall Woman*
Katherine Soniat, *Alluvial*

http://www.departments.bucknell.edu/univ_press

ALLUVIAL

Katherine Soniat

Lewisburg
Bucknell University Press
London: Associated University Presses

Associated University Presses
440 Forsgate Drive
Cranbury, NJ 08512

Associated University Presses
16 Barter Street
London WC1A 2AH, England

Associated University Presses
P.O. Box 338, Port Credit
Mississauga, Ontario
Canada L5G 4L8

The paper used in this publication meets requirements of the American National Standard for Permanence of Paper for Printed Library Materials Z39.48-1984.

Library of Congress Cataloging-in-Publication Data

Soniat, Katherine.
Alluvial / Katherine Soniat.
p. cm. — (Bucknell series in contemporary poetry)
ISBN 0-8387-5478-3 (alk. paper)
I. Title. II. Series.
PS3569.O65396 A79 2001
811'.54—dc21 00-034282

PRINTED IN THE UNITED STATES OF AMERICA

For Ashton and Shelton,
and for Pierce

In memory, for Robert

Collections of poems:

A Shared Life
Cracking Eggs
Winter Toys
Notes of Departure

Contents

Acknowledgments

Many thanks to the editors of the following journals in which these poems were first published;

Anthology of University of Southern California: "The Captain's Advice to Those Headed for the Trees: 1600 (an Ann Stanford Prize Winner); "Steward"
Anthology of Small Magazine Verse and Yearbook of American Poetry: "Fire"
Appalachee Quarterly: "Otherwise/ or Mrs. Herbert Jones, Tour Guide, Speaks of Mrs. John Rolf,1878"
Artemis: "A Retrospective: Portraits from A Private Collection"
Beloit Poetry Review: "Gens de Couleur: Ladies and Men"
Chesapeake Bay Foundation Magazine : "Oysterland"
Chicago Review: "Land Lights"
Controlled Burn: "Estuary"
Crazyhorse: "House of Cards," "Oil and Water"
Eureka Literary Review (ELM): "Coronation"
Georgia Review: "Razzy, Dazzy Turns to Jazz"
Hampden-Sydney Poetry Review: "Otherwise . . ."
Laurel Review: "Country Signs," "Powhatan Instructs His Councilor on His Trip to London,"
Licking River Review: "Primer in a One-Room Schoolhouse,"
Manoa: "The Landing," "The Beauties," "Naming It"
Maryland Review: "Oysterland,"
Maple Leaf Rag Anthology: "Storeyville, 1917"
Midwest Quarterly: "Fire"
Minnesota Review: "Brown vs. Board of Education Day"
New Virginia Review: "Selected Vocabulary: The Weroweance Speaks of Exchange"
Northeast : "The Priory Garden"
North American Review: " The Eel Hour"
Oxford American: "Alluvial"
Old Dominion Review: "The Sea Mark," "The Oils of Europe"
Poet Lore: "Along the Way,"
Prairie Schooner: "Fantasia," "Peter," "Hydra," "Eddying"

Quarterly Review of Light Verse: "The Moon Box"
Quarterly West: "A Country Grandson"
River Styx: "Dream's Landing"
Seattle Review: "Basso Continuo"
Shenandoah: "Child Care," "Two Daughters," "Journeying," "Forecast"
Southern Review: "The House on Royal Street," "Toppled Columns, Blue Sea and Sky," "Bronze John," "A Scrap of What the Yellow Fever Orphan Had to Say"
Southern Poetry Review: "Coming into the River Parishes"
Texas Review: "Hello and Goodbye on Miracle House Road"
Tulane Review: "Latitude"
Uncommon Place: Anthology of Contemporary Louisiana Poets: "Country Signs"
Wherever Home Begins Anthology (Orchard Press); "Forecast"
Witness: "Backtalk," "Hot Air," "Storeyville, 1917"
Yankee: "Gold"

Thanks to the Corporation of Yaddo and the MacDowell Colony for the residencies to complete this collection, and to the Virginia Commission for the Arts, Hollins University and to Virginia Polytechnic Institute and State University for research grants.

Special thanks to Mary Ellen and Steve Trimble for their domestic generosity: where it all began.

I have always known
That at last I would
Take this road, but yesterday
I did not know that it would be today.

—Narihira

ALLUVIAL

I

The Captain's Advice to Those Headed for the Trees: 1609

Lastly remember that faction, pride and security produce confusion; so the contraries well-practiced will make you happy.

—John Smith, *Travels and Works*

i. On Arrival

Come in off the tidal marsh, past the known
Sea of Virginia and you'll find a river
curving in a shimmery arc
like our moving, setting sun,
a mineral heat, the very gold of day.
Sail into those headwaters,
mindful of a deep draw for your barge.
Chilled air signals the elevated earth,
hillsides where you can peer down
upon the *naturals*,
be they of a beastly or human kind.
Responding to such loftiness,
they will look up to you with that certain fear
of the smaller for the larger, be it of true measure, or not.

ii. On Guardedness

When you see blue shade along the river,
deep coves of spruce and pine,
you'll be in the foothills of mountains
called the *Apalatsi*.
Wading from cold waters,
do not be numb to the uneasy state
of your barge tied surely to shore.
Store its sails and anchors near,
bedfellows for the dark.
They are the metal stays and billows of your divining rod:
the ship, our most blessed tool.

Recall there are those among you
who would steal her away, leaving comrades stranded
as birds in the thicket thorns.

iii. On Novelty

Search for what resembles most a clearing,
some thinning in the woods
where mulberry and her low cousins
range beneath the oak.
A cleansing of twenty acres a year
will be no small task.
There you'll come to know the foliage
as that of childhood hideouts,
but alive with eyes and arrows.
Even tall grasses offer a refuge
for these creeping spies,
each tree, but a watch tower full of malice.
For a brief time only will you be a thing of study,
of curiosity.

iv. On Exterior Expression

From their shrubbery, they will watch you
sweat, and harden, and chop
out a life of sorts.
Take care neither to show a face of sickness,
nor that more irksome one of fear.
Make your features stiff putty.
Those who lose such a visage should weep or vomit,
peering at the ground.
Turn the stoic's mask
on those figuring you from the trees,
and allow only the best marksman to pull his trigger.
That bullet must not be a wobbly spear
slung from chaos but one which arrives
unsuspected: a silver stopper to the heart.

v. On Natural Connection

Regard those you meet as kin to the land.
When the dirt you walk upon
becomes a good tint and texture,

look to each man and woman.
They bear evidence of the world
in their flesh—
that which is boggy and slick to the foot
breeds folk of puffed belly.
So when the high elm
and firm earth appear,
that tall tribe called Susquehanna
may stride forth—
clan and tree risen as if watered
on a summer day.

vi. On a Vast Darkness

Beyond your hard-won clearing
forests loom for the novice.
They hold no path with a charted meaning.
Perhaps, you'll wish for a guide other than our compass—
some makeshift Venus striding under the leaves,
like that star we looked to at sea.
Do not trust those who'll bow by day
and lead you dancing through the sun.
They'll loose treachery on you at night,
and probably not at all far from the place
you thought home.
Who among you was it that advised
we build an unwalled village
for fear of hurting these crafty ones' feelings?

vii. On Priorities

Once the trees are lain back to blue sky,
turn your ax toward building—
storehouse, the first to rise,
a space for August plenty.
Then see that public structures
go up before a single private house;
the welfare of the whole always central.
Select order over confusion;
if thoughtfully considered,
it is almost easy to do.

With houses set in a straight line,
streets designed with wide berth, men will have
a sense of welcome and cast off the inward.
Each thought carries them closer to town square.

viii. On Taking Advice

Lastly, and this image should dance
by day and follow you to sleep:
always, you are being meticulously
observed. Learn the eyes that travel
back and forth over your skin,
that want to grab and shake you by the scruff
till you let go their land.
To them, we're the plodding, dumb thinker
who takes each beginning as the first.
But why write home of discouragements
after crafting a fortress upriver,
uphill for hope?
Better the air be filled with smoke rings of man
upon man taught by survival.

Concerning Those of a Tender Education

Their ignorancies seem much more than all the true actors could by their experience present.

—*Travels and Works*

There are those trained to think of themselves
highly from birth,
those who cannot understand that savages and beasts
are our common plight
and, thus, make us of equal blood.
These are the stymied men, loud talkers of few acts,
who write home to bleat and wring their smooth hands,
astonished to find this fort no English city
with enclosures for dainty naps
or taverns to falsify the wearisome day.
They work for the private belly,
their heads lopsided with dreams of gold fallen magically
to the lap. Or then homesick, they plot to steal a ship
and float back to the pampering they think their due,
family stipend the goal.

The Oils of Europe

The fish chased Captain Smith, and on her tail was a poison stinger which she stuck an inch and one half into the wrist of his arm.

—*Travels and Works*

The task is always greater than conceived,
and so it was as we set sail to perform a discovery—
in and out of islands, coves, the wind so blustery
we named one land the Isle of Limbo, last howling
stop before Hell.
That morning when sun rose we saw
what natives most respected was a grazing of the marsh
with shot.
And, of course, they loved
our prized white beads, which caused great consternation
as gold does amongst the Christians.
The only glitter I saw was of fish so thick
we scooped them up with frying pans,
and that brings me to the Flapping One,
who speared my flesh with her sworded tail.
Swollen and blue, I commanded my grave be dug,
and stood therein, waiting, while the good doctor
rubbed me with all the oils of Europe.
Greased with such essence I came unpuffed,
and we dined on "enemy" for supper.
But first I gave that fish honors afforded the dead,
naming the isle Sting Ray to celebrate
yet another discovery— this time that I was
still most blessedly alive.

Coronation

Powhatan, neither knowing the majesty nor meaning of a Crown, nor bending of the knee, endured so many persuasions as tired us all.

—*Travels and Works*

Because Powhatan said he was King of the land
we named Virginia, we set forth to ensure him
he was Weroweance of All.
A bed and basin, fit for finest English gentry,
I commanded be displayed in his forest,
then a scarlet robe and crown of copper.
But this was no dress he understood,
nor could he see any reason to go down on bended knees,
except to get his brains thwacked out.
So our day progressed. We pushed down. He bore up,
until finally wearied, he stooped a bit,
and three of us quickly planted the crown and royal robes
upon him. At that, the barge fired salute,
and our new King, filled with fear, fled,
crown atilt, bed and basin pale amongst the trees.

Powhatan Instructs His Councilor on the Trip to London

First you go find John Smith. That done, find out if he is dead.
—*Travels and Works*

To judge the number of our enemy,
take a long stick to notch each time you see
one of those called English Man.
Then if you find our friend alive,
make him show you his god.
Probably it will appear something like a King James,
Queen Anne or a Prince Henry of whom he so often spoke.

See if it looks at all like the one we know,
his Admiral Newport of Virginia
since he calls him "father" and "king."
If indeed his god is akin to any of those mighties,
I will send pearl chains and years of corn blessings.
Far better than the white dog, copper crown
and bedstead he set out for me
so that I might sink to dreaming on my land.

Selected Vocabulary: The Weroweance Talks of Exchange

The subtle savage thus replied: "Even if your king have sent me presents, I am king, and this is my land."

—*Travels and Works*

You English approach like skinned moonlight
through the trees, raising thunder enough

to make ruin of our heavens, gods and stars—
osies, okes and pawpaxsoughes.

You have the cunning to learn our words
that address death and life—

righcomough, kekughes.
You turn them both to ashes,

then smile with a handful of beads
and whine out our sounds for "what can we eat?"

Do you truly expect the answer
to "where dwells Powhatan?"

We curl our lips up and back saying,
"in how many days will there come more English ships?"

You smile, we grin
and both of us know why

as you call out your prize phrase
to the one who'll save you time and again:

Kekutes, Pocohontas, or
"Bid Pocohontas bring baskets

and I will give her many white beads
to make her a chain."

Otherwise/or Mrs. Herbert Jones, Tour Guide, Speaks of Mrs. John Rolf, 1878

For twenty months, through Pocohontas's constant intervention, Jamestown stayed alive. Otherwise, life would have been unbearable, our drink was only water, our castles in the air (trees).

—*Travels and Work*

Here hangs the dePasse engraving of Mrs. John Rolf,
alias Rebecca, alias Pocohontas,
whose inscription states she was a native princess
transformed into John Rolf's wife
from the daughter of Powhatan, emperor of all
the tidal tribes of his land, otherwise called Virginia.

She's beautifully preserved in this 2 x 2 frame,
painted shortly after her kidnapping
and marriage,
shortly before her death in London
where she was brought to see the queen.

The face holds a gravity of expression
that usually comes with time.
Though Mrs. Rolf is only twenty,
she looks ruefully back.
In her vellum skin, there is only a small taint of copper;
an English ruff of the day surrounds her neck,
setting off the high cheek bones
common to that race.

The final blessing bestowed upon Pocohontas
Rebecca Rolf—called pagan by her husband—
was one of conversion: she died a Christian death
taken in by God in her new motherland.

Note the sensitive hands,
how she holds to those three ostrich feathers
as if they were her loved white beads
strung under trees, like chains of the moonlight.

The Sea Mark

Aloof, aloof; and come not near,
        the dangers do appear;
Which if my ruins had not been
        you had not seen:
I lie only upon this shelf
        to be a mark to all
        which on the same might fall,
That none may perish but myself.

If in or outward you be bound,
        do not forget to sound:
Neglect of what was cause of this
        and you will steer amiss.
The seas were calm, the wind was fair
that made me so secure,
        that now I must endure
All weathers be they fair or foul.

The Winters cold, and Summers heat
        alternately beat
Upon my bruised sides, that rue
        because too true
That no relief can ever come.
        But why should I despair
        being promised so fair
That there shall come a day of doom.

—the one poem written
  by Captain John Smith, 1630

The Earth Mark

Here lies one conquered who hath conquered Kings, Subdued larger territories and done things Which to the world impossible would seem.

—John Smith's epitaph, Saint Sepulchre Church, Lond(

(d. June 21, 16:

Away, away; three centuries
And sixty years this day
From when Earth began her damp rot of you.
Like your best suit of apparel
You too would fall in with orphaned things—
Saint Sepulchre, cold colony for the saved.
What would stay were your words
About "a virgin land, as if by art designed."

There you matched trees and animals with English names,
Familiarity embraced that made
The vastness less. A sailor's tale you spun of bruised
Landings, of coasts
Not to be sunk in time, but recalled as Sting Ray Isle,
Or that inland shade, Kynd Woman's Care.
You inked in the circumstance
Of foliage, of weathers cycling through the bay,

And in your one poem "The Sea Mark,"
I watched that shipwreck grow
Into our reminder of the low place
Of the grave:
Summer, Winter beat overhead,
Seasons collide and depart
Unchanged by the capsized men,
An ocean floor their final land secured.

—Miracle House, Chesapeake Bay
June 21, 1991

II

The Eel Hour

As if hearing a gravid Atlantic bell,
continent east, continent west,

eels rise for the autumnal dark of the moon
to journey up from sulphuric ground wells,

down the fresh-water creeks, through marsh and back
to an ocean deep enough to make their small eyes pop.

Gray skins refashion to sunset golds and purple.
They light the vegetable shade:

Sargasso Sea, that old stopper of wooden ships between
Kingdom of New Parrot and Continent of the Wise.

Into nests of eel-drift, these thinned swimmers
come to spawn and die.

Then the young return to land's beginning.
A dewy muscled slither mounts the humming dams,

curls through fields, drawn to their natal opposite—
artesian water, fresh and olive green.

Until the dark of the moon
throbs with *progeny, progeny,*

and again they flow down to the festive depths.

Dream's Landing

A neck of land on the Severn River,
four houses, stone chimneys, open pits to cook on,
and down the steep pine slope
where a schooner harbors at the dock.
The buoy's slow bong has called my father
back to where my mother was his bride,
the war not yet begun.

All afternoon he said he'd never find this place
from fifty years ago,
their rented house at Dream's Landing.
We drove the back roads of Annapolis,
up and down the river until he fumed, I quit,
and swung into a drive marked NO ACCESS
and I said, let's ask that man by the mail boxes.
Almost as he asked, the man nodded that indeed
he lived in old Doc Winters' place.

He and my father were making time,
talking about bottles and jugs of Juniper Tar Syrup
still piled high in the basement.
He had hit Dream's Landing, 1939.
But to me it was last summer
when I was the one lost in gallons of Louisiana rain,
looking for my mother's childhood house.
It was I who had given up
only to back into the sign,
Bella Vista, that lovely view,
a harder and harder thing to come by.

Country Signs

Another cloudy day on the Chesapeake.
June tractor plows, gulls drift in its wake.

I ride road swells like graves for the ocean's lost.
From chimneys, vultures survey the soy bean crop,

tendrils rooting down for damp connection.

✸

At noon, cows crowd the best tree on the land,
a shady spot across the road from Craddock Schoolhouse,

boarded up, still the imposing matron it was
in 1902. I drive slowly to hear the dry oats click

like little dice-tailed cats. And I'm still picturing
cats as I cross Kitten Branch Road.

✸

I take it as a country sign,
the way the lady in a blue shawl and the one in red

lean almost out of their lawn chairs
to whisper under a tree. They share

neighbors' secrets over baskets of shallots
for sale and scrubbed to pearl.

✸

It's meticulous work, weeding the floral rows
when all about the breeze is full of heated pine and lilac—

powdery greens, the ultra-violets.
My mother smiled and called it Rosy Future

as she spread that shade upon her lips.
I purse mine and lick, thinking back.

✸

Road dogs and fat wild berries
know the SLOW . . . CHILDREN warned of on the sign,

and that graveyard's filled with little ones,
their bones so many years past wishing.

How stiff the headstones look
near fields of windy green,

one great sprinkling apparatus crawling
high above the corn.

✸

On Old House Road a girl in tiger leotards
knocks at the back door with a bucket of day lilies,

hedge grown across the front,
windows boarded up far into summer.

Like anything with a past,
the whispering's almost sealed in.

✸

Reasons must have been good
for this village to be named Paramour, a duplicity of sorts,

and the next farm is Rural Felicity.
That's what I thought I had

until one morning my friend shook
her head and peered at me,

saying, *you look like you need something*
solid, handing me an ironstone mug

to hold to as I let myself down into this journey,
spider onto something by a thread.

✸

I swing into a cut-off, Chancetown Road,
then return to the thoroughfare,

wandering like these gulls,
a mixed-up, hoarding lot

full of farmers' seed.
Wavering above Pickpenny Neck,

one by one, they tilt and glide
back toward fish in the sea.

✸

Tough job, one man chopping at sunset
with a hoe. No gulls pursue him

with affectionate greed
or wheeling indifference.

It's him pulling his instrument
down through the air

into the clotted field.
And again.

The Moon Box

Summer lapses into sky and water
at Mrs. Moon's rented cottage
where I rise with the sun and hang on,

cloud-drift, to see as heron does.

All day I roll with the westerlies,
those pass-throughs of chill and heat
until, let down by moonrise,

I lie awake on the tidal bottoms:

2 a.m. drags me back across the granular,
then forward into randomness.
Forth and back, up and down,

a cloudskin of water, I'm ballast for the four winds.

Next day, on Old Claiborne Road,
the hound doesn't jump at me anymore,
does not even open an eye,

and when I walk into the corner post office,

the woman looks up to say,
oh, we've made up a new Moon-box
for you, as if I were about to birth

a celestial litter.

Journeying

First night of summer,
and the season's neither moon nor rain.
Who was it that cast me as a solitary?
The owl is agreeable, hoots *who*
with the wind.

Lean into me, I dreamed I heard you say.
Yesterday a hawk flew over,
talons heavy with prey.
I did not want its shadow to cross mine,
or you to touch me once, and not again.

Who ever finds the right space,
the soft spot with scrim across the pulsing?
Thin-skinned, a voice whispers,
and I think of you, hands out,
approaching that fluttery closing.

Primer in a One-Room School House

Thirteen windows on the water, pairs of cotton curtains
blowing in and out.

    Hold your chin up and face west.
    This is a room full of light,
    the place to start.
    A dayroom.

Nickel kettle and a standing lamp offer proof
against the dark, flag rustling at the doorway,
staunch as nineteenth-century skirts.

    Stand at attention, wandering thinker.
    Sometimes just sit up straight and
    see through the wind—

animal, vegetable and mineral,
our three kingdoms of choice.

    All of it questionable.
    Bristle for painting,
    bamboo for killing . . .
    if we look at them like that.
    Some days it's a task
    to direct the pointed things
    toward a benevolent end.

Hammering strikes up across the water,
pattern sinking in.

    A bit of what's to happen
    rests on the moment before,
    in what's going up and coming down.

Hello and Goodbye on Miracle House Road

Children whose parents had tuberculosis came by ferry from Baltimore to the Miracle House Preventorium where they were nourished to build up a healthy resistance.

The chapel is now a cottage—
altar changed to mantle, bedrooms built to the side,
and in the back of this piney lot
the one-room school house stands,
dormitories tumbled blazing into the bay years ago.

At sunset, the burned sleeping porch almost comes
dripping back. Bedtime words lift across the cots,
children and nesting birds listen to day's longest hour
as far away, the sick parent breathes on,
lungs shadowed with lesion.
Always this parent will be the branching,
departing one.

In her middle years,
a woman hears the twilight of early enchantment
and rolls over to sleep
where she meets herself as a girl on the ferry,
the homeland sinking away.
Her hand lifts with goodbye, or is it a greeting?
She's a toss of seasons, mist on her face
mixed with the body's most deep-down secretion.

The Preventorium

One room still bears the plaque,
"To a Happy, Healthy Childhood,"
meaning there'd be plenty to secure in the meanwhile.

Hand in hand, they came to feed off summer,
off frosted cakes, porridges and cream
to keep contagion away,
while tuberculosis filled a distant parent.

Among the potted dahlias on the porch table
sit two elastic waist bands—
the shorter marked *June*,
the longer, *September, 1939*.
Yellowed, they measure how a child grew sunny
and round, plumbed with health all her own.

Child Care

I promised God his fondest wish, anything he wanted
from a nine-year-old, if he'd just let me
move back home.

Bats fluttered over pumpkins in my school's Spook House
while my mother slept with her sick lung,
spit marked *sputum: positive.*
Contagion, month after month.

First her coughs had been called pleurisy,
then TB. Black umbrellas opened
up. A sanitarium
that's what they said our home would be,

and I went to live with friends
where I prayed hard to have her lungs scrubbed clean,
but she remained *positive,*
and every seven days she puffed up, withered,
then grew all over again.
Air treatments, they said.

She said the big needle in her stomach hurt
as they bicycle-pumped her up.
Clemy, the nurse, patted her slowly rising belly,
promising her lung only needed to float,
and rest.

I wondered why air needed to rest on air,
checking out books of x-rayed lungs.
All sacks of sadness to me,
the sickest ones, collapsed fruit on winter trees.

On week-end visits I surrounded our house
with my camera.
In the scrapbook there are seven shots,
seven angles of our house,
and under each is written:
I LIVE HERE.

Mercenary

I knew her as a woman in a white cotton dress,
seersucker when we moved to the south;
her last name was Adams; she came from a town
called Pine Bluff,
and for my first four years, she was paid to love
and sit me on the lap of her uniform.
Then one morning she was leaving,
moving on, she said, to care for an old lady
who lived in a big wooden house.
I rode in the backseat to deliver her,

to say good-bye to my lady. My Mrs. Adams
from Pine Bluff stepped from our car,
and I was reaching for her face as the door slammed
on my fingers. I saw a white house freeze
with its porch swing, potted flowers flaring
from pink to red.
I see it now like a snapshot injected with color,
something throbbing before going numb—
my fingers and my friend from Pine Bluff
vanished from sight.

Not even her first name got left behind.
I lifted my dinner plate from a table set for one,
went to her room with the radio
and bedded down with The Lone Ranger,
forking green beans into my mouth.
The William Tell Overture beat through the twilight,
as if she were there listening beside me
while a man's deep voice of concern
soothed his Indian companion,
and Silver and Scout galloped the canyon air.
I pictured this loyal group coming to carry me
to a height called Pine Bluff
as I lay in the lap of her white cotton sheets.

Peter

Ten miles north of Bachelor is the house
where my mother grew up. It took my growing up
to wonder how it was for her, dead this many years—
she'd left remnants, a firefly or two from the levee,
tales of the Granny who raised her
and thought "just like a man."

False River. *Bella Vista.*
I heard that place-name, the view described
with a *bella* that I'd always shifted into *buena*
to stop it from sounding bullish
and ratchety like war.

All the way from that spot on the map
I've gone looking for something of her past,
looking even to the two men
she spent two lives with.
Neither knew how she grew up.

Last winter, the first man,
my father, looked down at the linen table cloth
as I pursued her life, asking about the dead baby
that I'd found listed on my birth certificate:
"other pregnancy: one, born alive
but now dead." A child printed up
and given the quantity of "one."

An only-child, I asked of their first—boy or girl?
He looked away and said he did not recall,
knew only that it was buried in an unmarked grave
on the shores of the Severn.
I sat there hearing my mother
say how she'd wanted to name me Peter,
how she saw on me the hands and shoulders of a man.

Decoys

Under the flyway, my father and I drive the Eastern Shore.
I'm after fields of ancestry;
he wants me to see the hunters' decoys,
the thatched goose-pits at dawn.
I watch birds drawn to the lure of family.

Since he's still the father and I the old child,
we go through trying to be heard.
I say, *how about that for your next watercolor,*
the apple tree hung with winter fruit.
But he doesn't like to paint trees,
adds the sky's a dull wash of blue,
and what's more he can't do it from memory.

At night over dinner he asks how I write,
catch on to an idea.
Just watch it begin to move, I say,
my hand tossing the imaginary ivory
dice up before the candles.

Fire

like twilight makes one hesitate.
See the scalds on baby's hand,
that petal so easily darkened,

all our extremities diminished,
time felt finally as hooves
tamping down the dry savanna.

Nothing remains of what turned ashen
on the plains, no embers of that night
when flame first broke.

Sunset hues fade from ascendance,
as rock slams rock
until there were shadows enough

for the future and a past.

Backtalk

My mother was with me in the night. She would lie down beside me, get me to sleep, but long before I waked she was gone.

—Frederick Douglass

i. Mother

After those miles of dirt and field mice,
the darkness I went through,
I had the notion I could leave you the warmth of my body.
I was your ghost mother on a long chain,
arrived to sleep on my mama's floor.
By you. That close, so you would carry the heat of me
like a hand to the morning field.
You were the son I had to set aside,
miles from Great House Farm.
Your candlelight skin.
Six years you stayed away,
and I came to watch the stars,
follow them east to cradle you on that dirt floor.

ii. Son

In the end, I probably took my mother's death
as one of a stranger.
I hesitate
because there in my grandmother's cabin,
I laid up vague memories of her, sure as a coming rain
to the field. Some nights, late, she'd be there,
a hand traveling mine,
hers, the face I would never know as those in sunlight.
She was leg to my leg, finger to eyelid,
hum in my cold ear.
Friction and breath.
Then out she moved like the tide.
I'd waken on a cabin floor, look round
and round at the emptied morning light.

iii. Her Worldly Ghost Looks Back

Should I have told you ahead of the beastly
contradiction—the way they beat to hear a scream,
whip to make you hush?
Hands tied to the joist, stool kicked to the side:
you'd see it soon enough
in one eyeful of your auntie,
you peeking from the closet.
And you heard the absolute blue notes
that raked the piney woods on Allowance Day,
the human bottom a voice can scrape.
Oh, I watched your daily, hard lessons,
that cornmeal sack you slept in, headfirst,
your feet left out to split with frost;
oyster shell spoon of slop,
eat like a quick pig,
and if master called you bad
that marked you as tar on the fruit-yard fence.
Even your name became a reminder of our plight,
you "his little Freddie" to the young white Thomas.
I wondered a long time about that bread
in his Baltimore pantry.
You said it set you free—
you stealing food for the poor whites,
your "dear little fellows of Philpot Street."
Bribed with bread, they taught you the alphabet.
What was I to make of the so-called wand
you held between a thumb and two fingers.
I say it made you more like them.
Years later you wrote oh so sweetly
about white sails on the bay,
thinking it was cloth and a boat that made you wish:
Could I but swim! If I could fly!

And

The old cabin
with its rail floor upstairs
and its clay floor downstairs
and its windowless sides
and that most curious piece
the ladder stairway
and the hole curiously dug in front of the fireplace
beneath which grandmama placed sweet potatoes
to keep them from the frost,
this was MY HOME—
the only home I ever had,
and I love it,
and all connected with it.

—Frederick Douglass, *Narrative of the Life of Frederick Douglass*

Too Soon

God grant you find one face there you loved when all was young.
—Charles Kingsley

Once upon a realm of aqua, blues and greens,
the Faery Isle of Water Babies
bloomed beneath the horizon:

Small disconsolate ones, bruised by a master-race,
threw off their lungs to feel more fluid
life.

No longer the rough air to breathe,
no more a cheek to turn,
and never to be

Orphan Childe again,
little Moses laid down to want and wait
for one face to come back twice.

Who sensed his wet lament
but the paired geese
knowing no other,

down to the solo end?

Naming It

See your father squinting on the Pacific, the ships and uniforms lit in the glare. After that, you and I started from a dune, stars our backdrop, all the way to Key West.

—the mother

I was three when someone must have told
the war to stop, because a man called my father appeared
at our boarding house on the beach.
He was there and sudden and rushing through
my turret room, going for its five big windows
with the mattress my mother's cigarette had set afire.
Like a stuffed body, it crashed through the smoky night.

The war was still over when she woke me to get up
and go. Maybe my father had drifted back
to live on his ship, because she and I and
a Steve Sclafanides of Key West
were leaving, on our way to their "good new life."
In the backseat of the car, I cried
for a toy elephant, left in my big-windowed room.

I wondered if it were a war
or my lost elephant that was making me hurt like that.
Something was getting, had gotten, away.

I was after what Joe Gardner, the Englishman,
had had. He was the first name she was to marry.
The man before me, or my father.
He was the signal flag bracelet
I found at the bottom
of her jewelry box, saying I LOVE YOU.

He came before my father and his war
and Steve Sclafanides who went out, poof,
like a headlight, to be replaced
by Mr. Diboll of another town when we went that way.

The Beauties

Out of the seawall cracks, pink cosmos lean
with the wind
and, inland, mountains peak
                                                into thousands of feet of blue.
But changes came to the farmers of high crops
and to fishers along the coast—
                                    Havana with a new bidding to bow to.

Boys turned to men,
round stomachs flattened,
                                                then rounded again.
The old again,
a generation netted as crucifixes born with arms and legs.

Dark eyes blinked at the castanet's tiketa-tiketa-tik,
sunrise, a rouged tropic of cloud,
                        good-byes blown through breezeways of alleys.

But something closed its heart and walked out
on this city of the long *avenidas*.
I traveled them once
                                    at night as a child,
trolley rocking past the boulevard's royal palms.
We were the stick-folk then:
                                                my mother beside me
like a fraught statue riding a swath of light
to the end of the line.

From there I watched the colonial city
                                                            wobble its candelabra,
surf shaking the pier pilings beneath.
I looked up at her, then on to the sky.
She would not share
                                    her eyes with me.
The golden rumbling machine had left us
beyond *Esperanza, Santo Spiritus,*
                                                stops sung out along the way.

We were a duo, set out to try the single life,
stars swirled
                    round the whitewash of a city.
Sea-salt green underbellies flashed in the pier light.
I held to her hand
                    while about us swayed the deep, the high,
                                        and the far.

Steward

Today I saw the Christmas planet,
empty hornet nest high in a tulip poplar,
dried starpods circled around.

Drawn to the moon and sun,
we hoped to escape such darkness.
But we squandered the stroked-in treeline

and took lightly the shore's mineral shine,
the pebbled-hued clarity of streams.
Our globular home clouded. Hallways

through the woods widened and grew
quiet: A reliquary sacked.
No time left for the drowsy recitals,

the hums and hard work of late September.
No more practicing.
See the dirt on a cold blue sky.

The Cup

Underground springs on a curl,
then out in the bay,

over the waves
and down,
an oyster at rest in its shell.

Plump gray cleanser of water,
thousands of gallons

for thousands of years. And always
we thought the world our cup,
the fresh green heft of it,

sunglints at the bottom.
Then that spectacle was

almost all gone,
gotten away,
gotten way out of hand,

the farm-fed rivers flushing around
and around the bay:

this estuary
just another hole,
where the birds and beasts once came,

filled with marsh reeds collapsing.

Oysterland

Currently the oyster population of the Chesapeake Bay is about one percent of what it was in 1870.

—Bill Goldsborough, fisheries scientist

As a boy he heard the stillness,
the lap after his outboard stopped,
warblers in the marsh;
crabs almost too big for his net
speckled with sun underwater.

At low tide, oyster reefs rose
free from human curiousity,
free as the west wind that flew in
from the plains.

Now he studies water,
a man schooled in assault:
pantry reefs shrunk, the brood-stock nurseries
glowing emptier under each full moon.

The book in his lap is opened to 45,000 days ago,
photograph captioned, *1870 in Oysterland:*
an old man grinning on the bow of a skipjack
points to life in the bay.
The initial boy in both of them.

The Simple Weapons

Sleet on a boy's yellow slicker,
the trawler plunges through dolphin and shiners.
The sea has so much to offer and to startle.

If it's not an ocean that beckons, it's showers on a river
slipping birdlike through the tropics.
Parrots tilt brilliance above the fern,
a nod to afternoon in the leaves,
to feet padding below.

Boys glide the water, birds the air.
It was childhood for such a long while
until hand and eye came together
to subdue the horizon.

Latitude

Chilled June rain on Tanyard Road,
and I pick up a woman hefting groceries
back from Chance's Store.
Old and stooped, she grins, the rain's my blessing, mam.
Brought up from Florida to tend soy beans for the season,
she talks about how she coaxes them,
as if each were her own offshoot.
I let her out to resume her place in the drizzle.
The old school bus by their cinderblock dormitory
spends Sunday in a puddle,
migrants drawn to the glowing store.

✵

Mexican faces crowd together, their photo
on the front page of Water Times—
big smiles on the suddenly famous,
the infamously underpaid,
delivered to a promise land of crab picking,
bed and food on the Bay.
Told to keep to their rooms
and not to confound the locals by "speaking native."
Celebrities, they huddle over hampers of wriggling crabs,
the air, a startling geography.

✵

By noon, the rain's still a blessing pouring down
for those with callused hands and knees.
At Third Haven Meeting House,
the blue spruce drips outside a window.
Each man and woman bow in measured forgetfulness.
Pondered thoughts of private lives.
Nothing more to say, they find space for disappearance
in the irrigated quiet.

The Calvert Cliffs

Fog blurs the bluff's tall hollies, then drifts out to sea
where belief once reared its head as dragons,
sailors shouting at the next mirage.

Ambition had a long way to swell,
the nights and days it took to blow across an ocean,
the leagues stretched wondrously blue,

never like the task of return.
Ship by ship, staunch meanderers came to rest
on the bottom, strangers joined in the common-room of dying,

no matter how redemptive the horizon
once appeared.
I scoop handfuls of fossils and relics.

Bay burial dampens my palm.
Time has come like a burden gaining weight
to push all tenderness aside:

this land prepares a feast for the reminiscent eye
as if the fragmentary might reunite
to rise from my hand,

and the old world snort in the holly.

Hot Air

Growl all day and be dead tired at night,
the sign reads. Not this cat,
the world's every-cat purring on the landing.
A mole's black vestment hangs from her mouth,
sunset on her back,
the day an unpurchased time of grace.

It's out of kilter with the woman's bronzed arm
that reaches in the fish market,
forty-six bucks held up for four pieces of frozen sword.
And a helicopter dips over the town graveyard,
the week-end bank robber come
and gone to hide in the family plots.

City life has come to the charmed fishing village.
Turmoil arrived most everywhere,
the newspaper full of a midwest hamlet's story—
the wrecking ball mixed up City Hall
with an abandoned bakery,
and proceeded to knock it flat.

Restoration of this town rests
with a politician's wife raising funds
and cooing for "family values" out at Great Farm,
the plantation where Frederick Douglass
never caught a glimpse of his pale and ghostly father.
Our body politic continues to play its own fine fiddle
on Allowance Day,
and we do the prance of the faithfully misled.

Gold

Swans fly overhead,
a December of who-whos at dusk,

watery marmalade spilling from sandbar to sandbar.

Such afternoon amber turns talk
to Christmas feast
and guns to bring the wild fowl down.

Their shadows glide the blowing sunset marsh.

Cautionary, each tip of grass
lights a votive for the land.

The Landing

Bay full of sunlight, straight up and down,
with minnows shining. The ferry slip's great piles rot,
three on this side, three on that.

They embrace an emptiness the osprey weaves through.

I like to see her big wings beat
as she settles on the piling nest,
then peers about, sensing my shadow.

Osprey makes it look easy,

a mother who knows how to leave,
fly and go fish, then sprawl down
with her young again. I've tried

to learn the homing call, their high, then low notes.

She'll whistle back.
I play we're whistling swans,
thinking it would be a good voice to live by.

The two chicks hear my gawky song and hunker down,

preferring nothing
to one more foolish teakettle of a human.
I can't put my finger on it, but look at her.

Always she lights at some point higher than her young,

and when she looks down,
there seems an abiding steadiness to her head.
Porpoises dip around the ferry slip. My mother was one

who never got what she wanted, burial at sea.
She planned a transmigration,
setting aside water and the dolphin smile

to return in.

Some destinations are always withheld.
Always the future
we pinpoint our moves by.

I wanted another to go out looking with,

not for.
Solitary, we glide about in the abstract.
But these chicks are feathered bodies

rising out of the sticks.

One spreads wings like windblown paper ash.
She tries out her new weakness,
bouncing on pogo legs, then ducks,

some suddenness on the horizon.

From the bloodied morning feedings
to orange gobs of sundown, I've watched this nest,
wanting to see life ascend for the first time,

a move so old it's almost forgotten.

III

Alluvial

Pieces of levee towns swirl by,
batture farmyards drown in the river.

The stilt-house leans one day closer to the water,
its rooftop goat bleating about a place as old as spring.

Then fog settles in again
and tints with oil refinery fires,

like night-bombings wars and wars away.
In this confusion of twilights,

mist bathes each broken beginning.

Coming into the River Parishes

Under certain flood conditions in the 1800's, the Mississippi began to change its course and fill the shallow Atchafalaya, threatening to turn the land between Baton Rouge and New Orleans into a lagoon.

In north Louisiana
the place names grew out of change:

Hard Times, Water Proof, New Roads,
and the little lake-stop someone stepped out upon,

and called it Providence.
Then there's False River calling each assumption

into question.
To the south, waterways became amorphous in the marsh,

stream beds soothed into estuary, bayou and slough;
rivers rhythmic as the Comite, the Amite,

Tchefuncta and Bogafalaya,
and on aways to the Atchafalaya.

That's the one that almost missed becoming a river.
For years just a seasonal trickle

where the Mississippi dropped the left-overs of spring.

✸

Under thickets of magnolia,
vine-clog of scuppernong and muscadine,

fur-bearers prowled as the principal parties,
paddling through waters tinting from brown

to a pale clay-red.
Out of this confluence of color,

where the Red and the Mississippi met,
the Atchafalaya started to flow south;

this backwash a river to think about—
its waters deepening with gar and gaspergou

under a sky dark with duck.
Bullfrogs broached their bass song

for something old
in a world gone to change.

✸

It's hard to say
just how the world does change.

The old timer at the ESSO station
in Krotz Springs says he's seen it

come and go, swears the Atchafalaya
swam off with his childhood

as he watched the turn of the century
wheel in to the landing on French's Showboat

with its floating zoo of elephant, tiger and lion.
In their roar he heard the Earth

grow small,
could almost smell the diesel

soon to saturate the wind.
Shaking his head at "that river"

as if it were his own bad child,
he's gruff about the new-fangled locks

and levees that lay rivers to dry.
The ESSO sign's banging in the wind.

It's a toss up as to whose world
dries up and whose washes away.

The man points a finger,
laughs at the civil engineers

with their tools, up there measuring on the levee.
A trickle once deepened and, with no help

from them, the Atchafalaya rose
in the green magnolia shade.

Under the Street Lights

houses settle, and garden gates come to a rusty close.
The baby-rocking mothers,
the dreamless fathers,
their aging offspring tired of rain.
They nod off in a more northerly direction.

Spindly felines wander in and out of heat,
the housefolk gone, night arriving along the seawall
where one squall, then another blows in.

It's August or worse for a long time,
summer folded into a wilt of azaleas:
Flame, Orange Spike, and Lady Blush.
Hats on in the sunshine.
Bonnets off in the fall.

December passes for winter
and is called on only briefly—
tepid time that shifts like a cat
loose in one of its lost lives.

Forecast

Slow your stride in this city where streets sink
under curtains of rain
and balconies double as umbrellas.
Levees hold a comfortable irony, beginning six feet
below sea level.

Mornings thicken with rainy jasmine loaded onto sunshine.
Roasted coffee, molasses and beer quilt the lunch-hour whistle.
By evening, breeze washes in from the invariable south,
rippling the lake where schools of mullet browse
the surface like snakes in the bayou.

On the North Shore, turpentine groves bake
in the four o'clock shade,
while in mid-town stands one more attempt
at the above-ground:
those honeycombed stacks of graves,
always called the ovens.

Landlights

A child, I rode the air into town,
lights below prickling the bend in a river,

each home front ablaze
with what there'd be to remember.

Here lay my city of plaster saints
reddened in votive lights,

their arms held up to night-time
glut, and the aftermath of penance.

A landscape flickered of so much more than Jesus
and the weather to feel downright low about.

Or happy for,
barometric pressure working its swings

into the heart: midnight atwirl with street flutes,
feet tapping for silver coin.

Morning rains sheet the river bars,
outdoor markets slung with garlic chains,

a hex to cast out any devils,
while hail-Mary-full-of-grace rose through the drizzle,

sister-song of a fickle city.
But I was four and coasting down in a plane

to land on what I thought
was a flat, new world of companions.

I could not see my place set among the candles,
that city, my history of sundown.

Two Daughters

At length in February,
I wonder why I feel like nobody's daughter,
left with the pulse of a woman who was always headed away.
But today, mother, you
come back as the one left
homesick from birth—
your mother dead in the influenza of 1918,
leaving you to a Daddy with a big cigar
who handed you
                              over to your Granny,
and headed up east.
Your life stayed with her at Bella Vista
where you glued lightning bugs to your ears
and flitted the levee nights,
waiting for a Daddy to come blow smoke rings
and wink at you and Ida, your Granny,
who died when you were twelve,
leaving you
                    to her husband, Bough.
No one knows just how he disappeared.
He was the one you would point to in the album
peering from under his Panama hat.
Once you read the white ink on the black page
to me: Bough, the summer Ida
passed on.
                    That was the summer you gave up
her and the lightning bugs
as you were passed down-river to Marguerite,
the aunt who thought life was no place for school.
Life was tall and handsome. Laughing.
And soon she danced
                              you out of school,
over to France, then up to Devon
where I can hear you tell of strawberries

big as thumbs sucked down in whipping cream,
of the Englishman who spelled out
how he loved you in a bracelet of signal flags
while you danced yourself,
                                        careened yourself
into the arms of laughing men.
Here memory skips
over the thresholds of your departures.
It stops on me at sixteen,
you scoffing at my first love with *too dull, so serious.*
Now, listen to me, I'm your mother,
                                                                  aren't I?
We stood there staring,
as if this were revelation to us both.

Hydra

I still confuse her with the water,
far after our traipses along the seashore
following my father's Navy ship,
long after his return from the Pacific
to knock down my wartime solitude
of a mother-to-myself. Old story,

sad story where she remained fluid and
leaning over me like a spray
of night blooming flowers. Her scent would wake me,
and we were off to drive the coastline.
As one buoyant body, we followed his ship from port
to port until he cut us loose,

and we sank southward to the new husband
who could not keep her housed—
days, she walked the levee
to hear the Mississippi ripple and repeat.
The turbaned man, wrapped in a bed sheet,
held up a bamboo cross,
then dunked his people in the river.

She gazed, motherless from birth.
Water was her medium,
the heartbeat close and constant
that took her in.

Along the Way

That daily path through the flowers to the stucco school
seemed all of a piece.
          At my approach, moths flew from the drooping althea,
pavement cracks thickened with moss.
Across the drainage ditch, across the street,
the city block changed
                    to a tangle of palmetto,

and behind that stood the house clumped in shade
of another time.
I knew its story: an old brother and sister lived there,
their faces shrunk
          to cameos behind the swimmy window glass.

Approaching it,
          I made ghost-runs in the trade winds of a city,
                    drawn to a revolving door of spirits,
something forgotten and unmothered wavering
toward a shape.

Dropping back through the decades,
I'd play I was the mother on their porch,
                    calling, it's time to come back.
Time never does come back, and neither did my mother,
and I went on pretending not to care,
          heading west through the sodden, purpling althea
on my way to school.

There was no rising out of that landscape,
no next state.
          Only neighbors talking about the man and woman
                    waiting, some said, by the window with a gun.
The grown-ups whispered.
I imagined,
                    and the two old people kept vanishing
deeper into that house's silences.

Little came or went
except my thoughts that darted like chameleons.
                                        Once a dog howled at twilight near the house.
I pictured alarm scuttling through the brush,
rehearsing my own expectations.

This was early history,
my first idea of history—
                                                child wandering through the trees,
          a man and a woman at the window with a gun.

A Retrospective: Portraits from a Private Collection

At the beginning, no whistle rises from a river boat.
There is "Henry Durell III," done up and framed in 1710.

In white knee breeches, he struts about the South
with a falcon on his fist and a black boy at his feet

whose white-eyed, worshipful look is a paradigm.
He's the first slave painted in America,

and perhaps he's the reason why the likes of Henry
and his falcon stayed on for the next century,

for a time when the Civil War was ripe for canvas.
Its roots were still sunk in the cotton field

when somebody got busy painting "The Breakdown,"
dance of a grinning cabin boy, harmonica

honking to his feet. He must be looking forward
to "Sunrise at Fort Sumpter, 1864,"

hung to the right of "Portrait of a Gentleman,"
subject unknown, but familiar: that saintly,

anonymous look from too many benedictions with wine.
It's almost evening in his South,

and the gentleman is comfortably at home,
before home disappeared and the South gave up

the cabins of happy dancing feet
it had a hard time painting into place.

The House on Royal Street

One possible explanation of Madame Lalaurie's perversions was that her mother who helped start first black school in New Orleans (c. 1800) had been murdered in a black uprising.

—Deirdre Stanforth

The good lady, Madame Lalaurie, kept her mouth shut.
She kept the third-floor attic locked.
But still their voices squeezed out.
One neighbor saw the small black girl
chased across the courtyard,
Madame with a whip at her heels.
The neighbor heard two sets of feet flying
up the three flights of stairs.
She watched the smile glide across Madame Lalaurie's face
as her whip curled from the steep-pitched roof,
and a child disappeared.

Then there was quiet.
The authorities nodded to the details of "property abuse."
They listened to what the neighbors told,
and still reports of whips and cries came out,
and Madame continued her Sunday rides
with a coachman dressed in royal purple.

All smiles and the perfect gait.
She needed Sunday to appear this way.
She needed those parasoled rides
after the "rooftop incident,"
wanted them after the late-night dinners
when politely she would lay her napkin down,
excuse herself to attend the seven slaves
she kept alive and collared to the attic walls—
beatings she'd deliver,
guests told of whippings after walnuts and wine.

This was the setting
for what the neighbors heard and
told. Told and heard.
This was the circumstance
that one April day the cook struck a match to—
this house on Royal Street that held the kitchen
the cook was chained to
and took a match to,
one last long blue sigh rising out of the flames
as neighbors climbed the stairs
to those they found chained
in an art of malformation.

Flames leapt, and the coachman's purple
flashed through the courtyard gate,
Madame gesturing in the backseat
as if whipping horses into froth.
Those two clattered away from their history
in a place where no one did a thing.

Gens de Couleur Libres: Ladies and Men

As successive generations of lighter colored women were born, resentment began to appear. By 1778 these women numbered 1500, most of them unmarried, all free and kept in little houses near the ramparts.

—Harnett Kane

Was she $\frac{1}{2}$, $\frac{3}{4}$ or $\frac{7}{8}$ white,
and was her descriptive *mulatto, quadroon oroctoroon*
or was it *tieceron, griffe, marabon, sacaron* or *os rouge*?
And why is it when the word quadroon comes up,
one rarely thinks of males?

For there was a brother
as sister stepped out for The Quadroon Ball.
Though brother would probably be growing tall
upriver where his Daddy'd sent him
to make sure he found a woman darker than himself.

Sister went on dancing, spinning the ballroom floor.
A touring Englishman took note
of "that peach-soft, velvet-brown quadroon
with the dark, liquid eyes and perfect gait,"
remarking on "the notable progress
she'd made toward joining a superior race."

And indeed she became superior,
parading the city in her plumed carriage, bonnet
and jewels: white Wife glared, vowing her husband
had had no part in that,
and sister swore that her lover never, ever
would depart.

So it went in the little houses near the ramparts,
and brother kept writing from the country,
wondering about home,
and the Wives kept on getting redder,
angrier until finally law forbade

"any free woman of color from acting white,"
banishing all silks, sapphires and the regal hats.
Little could be done about the dark, sad eyes
when these women were released
"from the privilege of serving as a white man's mistress."

She was a lover retired
perhaps to own a rooming house
"to accommodate tired gentlemen."
There we could find sister, a little older,
proprietress of a house of linens.
Mornings, she smiles pretty;
sundown, she draws man-sized tubs of flower water,
while miles away, brother's out of sight
and marrying back his skin.

The Priory Garden

Hummingbirds celebrate in the gentian petals,
holding their own
two inches of the world
                    in a wing-throb.
Not the black bumblebee,
but all its motion.
            These birds hammer their midget hearts,
air traveling the rapidly vanishing wings.
Breath cast keys up on the scale
from the vespers choir
chanting low notes
of the Misereri.

Selecting Thoughts for Rouen

Sister Madeleine was in the group of Ursuline nuns who were the first educators to arrive in New Orleans (1730). They built Ursuline Convent, the oldest standing building in the Mississippi Valley.

By December, the light dried out a bit,
and my eyes had more to do than look inward:
Rouen lay behind
as we seven sisters of Saint Ursula sailed off
to carry our world across months of ocean,
then up a river's mouth,
each of us perched atop of the pirogue's luggage.
We wobbled forth to regain our life of absences

in a setting God congealed from the marsh.
Slowly, the Convent walls went up,
white-wash summering into green.
Like heathen river spirits,
lewd cries from the streets rifled the altar quiet.

I tried to make glory out of gloom,
penning letters home to Rouen,
missives with news of the finest pumpkins, figs and swan.
For pure mischief I added a splash of salmon,
telling tales on a people whose daily sacrifice
was to feed their children hominy and fish grease
so they might afford the plushest Christmas brocades.
God had me see a mind ignorant of salvation,
but expert at display.

I chose not to write of those days on the stormy Atlantic.
Weeks with fifty chickens and forty sheep
flopping to their seasick deaths;
nights when only ropes could sooth us
in the heaving bunks—
confusion such that not one of us could design
a string of words a saint would listen to.

Bronze John

Walking my nightly rounds, I saw flames of burning tar that illumined the streets and river so that I could see as in daylight. Through windows was flung this sickly flickering; persons could be seen struggling in death alongside blackened corpses.

—Reverand Clapp's diary, 1853

What does a sky like this mean,
this lowering dark
that neither tar soot nor cannon blast can alleviate?

The yellow-fever sky rains down again,
a curtain corpses pile behind at the cemetery gates
while the nicknamed death, Bronze John,

comes to rock and nod on a summer visit—
10,000 dead by September.
What does deluge and decay mean to a city

where all but the dead abandon neighborhood infirmaries?
The fever lurks in puddles under every house,
hatches in cisterns, in open ditches filled with the city slops.

Mosquitoes whine a dirge in bed-netting all night.
Townfolk smile and swat away "just another household pest."
They think they know the cause—

one day it comes from houses rife with "rotten wood,"
the next, it has to be "tiny flecks thickening the air."
And they think they, the Creoles, are immune,

that this is a plague designed for Irish riff-raff,
for sailors snoring one off in the river-front boarding houses.
It's a disease of filth risen from the marshlands

where Germans and Italians breed.
Surely it ripens only among these pockets of outlanders.
Then why does the sky overwhelm and stay black,

and why do the multitudes' bodies bronze,
then darken overnight?
One comes to see there are no prearranged terms

for a sickly season.
Carts swarm the muddy road leading north
to towns that will not let them in.

Faces continue to distend,
each realizing its own untailored death
that all the limewater, razors, opium,

and onions in a shoe cannot dissuade.
On balconies, brothers spin gambling wheels
and bet on who's in the approaching funeral cortege.

Bodies rot, are burned.
Coffins rise from the sodden ground.
The dead throw off their covers, return to face

the hysterical living living through a plague.

A Scrap of What the Yellow Fever Orphan Had to Say

My dear fathe,
I love you with all my hearth.
And you did died so quick
And I think I see you always
And I which you were life
You were so good
Our hole famely were . . .

Razzy, Dazzy Turns to Jazz: 1900

Raddy, taddy dirty notes
drifting off Perdido Street,
mud route leading from downtown

out to the dank, dark swamp
where there's a sludge so low down

only a let-loose, bawdy-house sound'll pull you out:
Elemental, syncopated, that fine old Tiger Rag
basted together from a work song of rice sacks

stacked upon the back,
backcracking tunes tossed with the rhythms

of the Gombo dialect, and a tad of aria thrown in.
And there you've got it.
You can get it

at The Come Clean and Funky Butt Barroom.
You can spot it in the lanky moves

of The Razzy, Dazzy Spasm Band
with Elgin movement ticking in their hips
and a twenty-year guarantee.

They're the ones that got folks to rhyming
till "razzy, dazzy" slid to *jazz*.

You could see it being born in Stale Bread Charlie,
tapping and moaning on his lead pipe;
notes lush and full

flying from Warm Gravy, Whiskey, Monk
and Mr. Chinee. That whole band

with it, following and holding, then letting it
all tumble loose, with a kettle for percussion,
half-barrel for the bass.

while they sat a-spasming, a-razzy dazzy jazzing 'em
with cowbells and a rattling gourd of rocks—

sweet sounds that keep up
to near dawn, and won't stop till every fancy man's
brought swaying to his knees,

a believer on Perdido,
swamp route for the lost.

Storeyville, November 12, 1917: Midnight

By order of the U.S. Navy,
prostitution was hereby declared illegal.

Women cart off what they can.
Boston Terrier on a leash, bird cage in the hand,
feather mattress on the back.

It's a losing game for the owner of the house.
Someone breathed stale breath across all the mirrored
ceilings, the walls—once done up with English shepherds,
solemn presidents, and Shakespeare—
now stripped clean.

Tonight, it's a withering of Kate Townsend's
where flowers hang from tester beds
and rose water ripples the inlaid gold
of chamber pots.

It's a comeuppance for Minnie Haha
whose makeshift family stares, framed above her bed,
brass plaque entitled Mr. and Mrs. Hiawatha.

And the race is over to see
who will be the first to bed down the new girl,
an exotic part-this and half-that.

All over for 190,000 brothels spread across town,
over for the singled-roofed ones that holds 20 "cribs"
where a woman and her bed
go for $3.00.

Old trade wanders Basin Street, more than one girl
struggles with a carpet on her back.
She's never seen a mirrored ceiling
or met Shakespeare in the parlor.
Her price has always been a quarter.

The Country Grandson, 1920

My first Mardi Gras.
The church bells started their slow bong.
I counted eight as Robert, Grandfather's man,
took me by the hand, led me down the damp alley.
The courtyard's iron gate banged behind us.
On a balcony, a man was singing to his parrot in the sun.
Garbage floated by in the ditch.
I took one deep breath, and held it
till I couldn't anymore.

At The Corner Costume Shop
we stood in line behind two billowy nuns
wobbling like sails of navy blue and white.
The cash-register lady grinned when one asked for
a devil suit in the largest size.
They had no imp suit small enough for me,
so Robert spotted a black cape and hat
he called Boy Witch,
and rented himself the last of the big red devils.

We walked through morning stink
to find what Robert promised would be King of the Blacks:
King Zulu and his banana-wagon parade.
I held tight to my friend's red-mittened hand,
my pointy witch hat tilting through the crowd,
the wind wet like back home in the country,
Summer rain coming through the field.

The crowds' voice sounded like that,
going from soft to loud with *here comes the King!*
Robert lifted me to his shoulders as the river barge
pulled in, and King bowed from his bamboo throne,
then waved the broomstick scepter,
topped with a big stuffed rooster.

I yelled to Robert to wiggle hello with his devil horns.
The king winked right at me,
clucked to his rooster,
and with a jerk, his mules clopped off, and
wagon # 2 rattled up—the end of his parade.
There, a granny-lady rode like a queen,
her white hair glittering with sequined roses,
tubs of iced fish at her feet.
Scales flashed as she cleaned, cooked,
and threw fried fish through the air.
Crisp slices flew to the crowd, and up to the wagon of her king.
I wished hard to catch one

but we walked on down the dirt street,
past rows of little houses with girl-names
painted above the screen doors—
words Robert called out as Chicago May
or French Marie. The real Anna Wanda he pointed to
as she pulled at her stockings on the door stoop
of The High Brown Social and Athletic Club.
I asked him to say that name twice for me,
while the two of us kept winding from paved
to muddy streets, and on into the setting sun.

Gutter Bird

Wisteria and wine.
A parakeet tipples from the gold goblet rim.

Past the courtyard gate,
a beggar chants her charms again.
She squats on the curb,
pops red grapes into her mouth
and spits at the dead rooster
with a yellow rose tied around his feet—

spell cast on what is
perhaps her last supper, or first in days.

Words the White Man Use

In the middle of the book, *Fabulous Cresent City,*
it's late on Mardi Gras Day, 1922,
when the terms of the story
                start to change,
the author acknowledging the man mixing drinks
for King Zulu who reigns in a back-town bar.
                Ice clinks and that bartender turns
sleek, then deepens to *blue-black*
as customers jam together, an *animal huddle* in the den.
They watch women who don't dance,
                but *lunge their hips*,
skin colored into those *nice paper-bag shades*
ranging from *high yellow* down to the *dusky octoroon.*
And there's a pale one in the short red skirt
lolling on the King's lap.
Her scent
        is part of the *stench of unwashed bodies*,
        bodies equipped with *fine white teeth*
        like those flashing from the thin *quadroon*
who now squirms her way toward the king.
All this lolling and lunging just before the chairs
begin to fly, and King's off his seat of honor
to greet the brawl at hand.

That's it for Mardi Gras in a bar with King Zulu.
The story shifts
                to another spot in town,
The Ramos Bar off the marble lobby of an old hotel.
Bartenders in one immaculate line
jiggle silver shakers of Gin Fizz.
                They sound a rhythmic beat,
quite uninvolved with lunging.
Fizzes froth with beaten egg whites
for a lady at the bar,
                orchids looped about her throat.

Her smile's in place,
her hips are quiet.
                                        They remain on the stool,
and there is no name for the pigment of her skin.

Brown vs. Board of Education Day

I dressed in pique, and carried daisies
in damp newspaper as we drove off to flower
the statue of John McDonough,
the man who founded the big stucco schools,
McDonough #1, #2, #3, and all the way up to the teens.

Each spring we paid homage to the king of schools,
our bus fuming toward the park by City Hall
where we laid limp flowers at McDonough's cement feet,
our skins pearling with sweat.

Behind us, ten blocks from our school,
there was another class of children just like me.
Unlike me, they did not dress in white,
nor did they come to praise John McDonough's feet—
these small people, part of the *thems*
soon to be loosed on the *us's*.

That's what I heard the grown-ups say
on the porch the summer of '54. They scowled.
The wooden swing creaked, and I wondered
about that word they kept using, *different*.
These were a different people.
But somehow not different like white kids
living in stilt-houses on the levee:

Year after year, we sat, wooden desk to desk,
in one classroom;
their river wrecks and floods,
barnyards moving into the kitchen
were tales far better than history.

And each McDonough Day the school bus swerved
us all along, a scrubbed and chloroxed load
that chorused our mixed-up version
of "Columbus, Gem of the Ocean,"
thinking it took three ships and a tune
to discover a whole new side of the world.

Approaching a Summer Scene

At best, some form of revelation must be at hand
as I drive into the outskirts of a city
where every billboard hawks mental health clinics
or a frosty bottle of Bacardi Breeze—
pineapple juice and rum contend with the other signs
that try to get serious in big letters,
declaring LITERACY NOW.
Half crazy or drunk, who wants to read a book?

But someone wants a room in the cinderblock motel
whose marquee reads ROOMS BY HALF HOUR,
and the very thought of what might result from that
has the state legislature up in arms:
senator vowing on the radio that sure women have
a "choice," and he's there to make sure that choice
will be for LIFE:
Breath To All Babies Born From Incest Or From Rape.

A few stations over, a disc jockey screams
the politicians think that he's a dirty Commie,
and they jammed the air waves
just as he was giving his thoughts against
their censoring CDs.
Yep, he says, his voice just up and vanished,
but don't you worry, he's back now to praise Arkansas
where a black beat the American Nazi Party candidate,

while in Louisiana they're voting in a Klansmen
and pounding flag-burners,
thanks to the new-and-improved misdemeanor law:
For a $25 fine you can knock the hell out of
just about anyone you please.
With a retiring grunt, he punctuates what he thinks
of freedom of expression.

I am seeing freedom on the loose.
The uncut median on the highway burgeons
with a public crop of corn,
and on a side street things are going at a weird tilt.
One man mows the front lawn
and drags along his poodle on a leash
while clutching a bouquet.

Singlehandedly, he's pushing hard
through the tall grass.
His wife peeks from the window
at what's left of a dog and his man
bearing flowers through a hot summer day.

Toppled Columns, Blue Sky and Sea

Greek sailors work the longitudes to a gangplank
on Decatur where the women wait.

The Acropolis Bar's sign lights up,
columns toppling beneath an Aegean sky—

the blue sky of Plato hangs adrift
in a city that rises on a shot of sloe gin

and dozes while bars exude a sorry music,
so homesick it drags the fog

for Greeks,
draws them to the late-faced women,

lips fluent with ouzo, bouzouke,
words easy as the hometown tongue

of *boid* and *foist*. First birdsong,
when the streets come clean with sun,

upright till night falls black, then blue
and neoned above a woman with the swollen arm

who beckons. She sings loose-talk in the wind—
all the exiled loose in a broth of fast and glut,

of garlic and magnolia mixed in the same sour breath.
Here, our lady of the Acropolis waves

from under her sign of ruins.
The Greeks roam Decatur,

pockets full from the sea,
heavy with what the sea comes to mean.

Eddying

It was a rare day when she spoke
of her childhood,

but that recurring dream
held something of the unspoken in tact.

I see her, sitting on the morning porch,
passing it on.

How last night, the river called her out
to swim again,

and now it had reshaped to a harmless, daylit thing.
But in the dark, she'd been with it

and in it,
washing into those pixie men

whose naked thighs squeezed
the twigs they rode,

whose cold spears showered her
as she swirled in the muddy current.

That water must have been an alleyway
she peered down, then rushed down,

hoping the sun would offer safe exit.
And always, the next day she told me the dream

as if I were her dead mother
returned to soothe her child

in the damp summer sheets—
that twilight she went into and

came out of, trying to make sense of.

Oil and Water

She could keep the secret of her birthplace only so long,
and she's probably nodding now
at the movement in these telephone wires—
my call, the receiver picked up,
house directions from a cousin
zipping through the swelter.

Setting off with maps leading to Bella Vista,
I drive miles north
to stop at a liquor store for more directions.
An old man points me off toward False River
with his brown-bag pint,
off past a school bus of women headed upriver
to see their prison men.

The clouds are black,
wind bending cotton crops along the spillway.
Hail, skylights, an ocean lets loose.
I'm miles past False River,
passing four times the same boarded-up mill.
Up and down the road I go,
under an orange light swinging caution into the deluge.

Giving up, I back into a shell drive,
hit an incinerator oil-drum.
My tail light reddens the skull and crossbones
stamped on this can of gloom.
Above it, the sign Bella Vista sways in a tree.
I take the flooded gravel drive
to be greeted by my cousin with a candle at the door,
central hallway behind her thick with mist.
Lights blown out,
air conditioning meets the stormy warmth.

Through the afternoon I peer at candlelit photographs,
yellowed people, rooms, boxes of old letters.

Then with a few mute decades in mind, I leave,
the air outside sunk to winter chill.
Driving fast toward June,
I see the blackness slip into the rearview,
and, without pause,
I'm back in the tropics of day after day.

Fantasia with Love and Death in the Wings

If these dead were on the long flight
down to the grave,
I would stand at the foot of the stairs
with a silver tray of poppies,
saying, eat, this will lighten the body.

But these specters are making their way up,
out of the night-bin.
They've come for thick bread and butter,
for the dawns insomniacs dwell on.

See how they crowd and are remote,
restless for this world—
lamps and oil,
clocks that chime dream into logic.

No longer loquacious, they murmur,
and I stand fast, an usher for their longings.
They are giddy with access and need
direction—
to my right is the sickroom,
where someone keeps on dying.
To the left hangs the crotch-smell,
the room of a man and woman
forever young and coupling.

They have it in them they'll be leaving.
On the landing my guests hesitate.
For now, we take each other in,
listen.

Basso Continuo

is wet land and the river
that makes high tide out of spring—

goat on the stilt-house roof,
ripples lapping the floorboards

as a cockroach flies from one screen to another,
its wings a wild card caught in the shuffle.

Down the road, a house done up in parlor chintz
whines into the early hours

with some dead baby's ghost.
What fit this land-of-sorts

with a brain-of-sorts?
Rainy atmosphere marbleizes into myth,

clouds fatten on the river.
A god of cumulus presides

over marsh that flies sunset as warning,
over lizards that bloat their throats

at levees meant to hold.

House of Cards

In the dirt
is where my dime store turtle ended up,
the painted palm tree poisoning his shell.
I wrapped it round and round in tissue,
then lowered the burial jelly jar,
earth, one dark wet landing
with more underneath.
                                        Azaleas
drooped in the heat,
July stifling my forays to the pantry
to dip fingers in mason jars of fermenting,
brandied peaches.
Years from then, the notion of warm preserves, pantries
and gusty central hallways
seems extinct—
that tunnel the attic fan breathed through,
where voices spoke low and the bedrooms branched;
where telephone table held the blue enamel lamp
painted with Japanese women huddled under umbrellas.
My realm of rain in their garden of blue.
That too would disappear
                                            like the attic stairs
leading up from the sleeping-porch
to the mail-order printing press.
There we grouped and cranked out childish news,
believing the bits of our days flew,
needed, into the neighborhood
                                              while the lattice
under the front porch went to rot,
a crawlspace smelling of turtles in their death regalia,
the sodden earth trying hard to generalize, eat away
our threaded tapestries.
                                      Over the summer

the air took a turn,
sank from the cushion in the window seat.
The sky enlarged to rainy purple.
Next door, the tin garage continued
holding our curtained galas of "Rapunzel,
the Magic Maid."
                                        After the play,
after another winter, we climbed the last
of our rooftops, setting the April sky ablaze
with Japanese plums,
thunks echoing from garage to garage.
My first alarm with an armored sound.
I thought of pale gardens
                              where umbrellas proceeded to go up,
the intricate passages of houses come down.